World War Two

The English Reading Tree

Published by G-L-R (Great Little Read)

Written by Keith Goodman

This book has been written for children aged seven and over, and it is part of the English Reading Tree Series.

Your child will be able to read the majority of words, but those that cause difficulty should be read together and pronounced slowly.

This is the perfect tool for parents to get their children into the habit of reading and focusing them on how words are formulated and used within simple sentences.

If a word does cause difficulties, make sure to re-read the sentence containing it, again, and go through the meaning if necessary.

Here is a fun activity before you start to read

How many things do you know about WW2?

1 What date did Britain declare war on Germany?

2 What was the name of the British 'War' Prime Minister?

3 When did the Japanese attack Pearl Harbor?

4 Which Allied troops fought in the Battle of the Bulge?

5 What was a Liberty Steak?

6 Which two countries fought in the Battle of Iwo Jima?

7 What was Enola Gay?

8 What is significant about May 2, 1945?

Table of Contents

The Start of World War Two

The deadliest war ever was the Second World War (WW2).

Most of the countries on the planet were involved in some way. Over 70 million people lost their lives as a result of this conflict and these included civilians as well as soldiers.

WW2 involved on the one side the Axis countries of Germany, Italy and Japan and on the other, the four main allies of Britain, France, America and the Soviet Union.

On September 3, 1939, Britain and France declared war on Germany after German troops invaded Poland.

The European part of the war ended on May 8, 1945, with the German surrender.

The Pacific War ended September 2, 1945, with the surrender of Japan.

Even though the war started in Europe, it had soon spread to other regions of the world. A huge part of the fighting took place in Southeast Asia.

German troops invade Poland, and the war begins.

What Caused the Second World War?

Just like the previous world war that took place from 1914 to 1918, the start of WW2 was caused by many factors. However, the peace terms and the subsequent heavy price paid by Germany after the First World War was one of the main reasons.

The Treaty of Versailles

This was the notorious settlement that was extremely harsh on the German nation. Germany was blamed 100 percent for World War One, and forced to pay huge sums of money for the damage caused by the fighting. The Treaty of Versailles destroyed the Economy of Germany and left the population without money to buy even basic food to survive. Over the years, the Germans began to believe that they had been 'stabbed-in-the-back' and that they had not actually lost the First World War. This myth was helped by the fact that the allies had stopped short of invading Germany at the end of WW1.

The Rise of Japan

In the 1930s, Japan was becoming very strong economically and wanted to expand its influence in Asia. In 1931, it invaded Manchuria, and then in 1937, overrun the weak Chinese nation.

Fascism

In the period before the Second World War, some European countries became fascist and had at their head, fascist dictators. The first fascist country was Spain, which was ruled by General Franco. In Italy, the fascist dictator, Mussolini, gained power, and in Germany, Hitler became the Chancellor. It was Mussolini in particular who wanted Italy to have an empire. He invaded Ethiopia in 1935. A few years later, Hitler would start to expand Germany.

Hitler's Plan

Hitler stormed to power with promises to make the nation great again. He became Fuhrer (Chief) in 1934 and recognized the weakness of the global powers such as France, Britain, and Russia. He began to arm the nation, which was against the peace terms of the

Treaty of Versailles. He made an alliance with Italy and joined with Austria.

Nobody did anything to stop Germany, and so Hitler became braver. He invaded Czechoslovakia in 1939 on the pretext that Germans were getting discriminated against.

The rise of Hitler and Fascism in Germany

The policy of appeasement

None of the big powers wanted another war and tried to keep the peace by doing nothing. They reasoned that if they did nothing that Germany would stop its expansion. This only made Germany more aggressive, and in the end, war became unavoidable. Poland was the 'red-line-in-the sand,' and Hitler crossed it.

Trivia

In the early 1930s, there was a big economic crisis, and many people all over the world were starving. The war changed all of that, and industry began to boom as they worked overtime to make guns, bombs, planes and all of the necessary materials that accompanied conflict.

As in WW1, America tried to remain neutral.

The Two Sides

Britain, France, Russia and America were the Allies.

The British Prime Minister for most of the war years was Winston Churchill.

He was well-known for his inspiring speeches and was a great politician who became a British Icon.

Franklin D Roosevelt was considered by many to be one of the best American Presidents.

He was the leader who guided the USA through the Great Depression and then into the Second World War.

Russia was led by the ruthless dictator, Joseph Stalin.

Of all of the Allied Countries, Russia suffered most, and the Eastern Front saw some of the hardest fought battles.

When the war was over, Stalin set up the Eastern Block and built the Berlin Wall.

Charles de Gaulle was the French leader.

The Allied leaders met during the war to decide of strategy.

Stalin, Roosevelt, and Churchill

The Axis Alliance was formed in 1936 between Italy and Germany. In 1936, there was an anti-communist alliance signed between Germany and Japan.

The Pact of Steel was agreed between Germany and Italy in 1939. Japan joined the pact in 1940.

The three countries that made up the Axis were all ruled by dictators.

In Germany, Adolph Hitler wanted to fulfill his ambition of joining all German-speaking nations and controlling Europe from Berlin.

Mussolini controlled Italy and was the leader that ultimately inspired Hitler. He had ambitions to create the next Roman Empire.

Hitler and Mussolini

Emperor Hirohito was the head of Japan from 1926 until 1989. He was the only one of the three dictators that survived the war.

Dunkirk

The advance of German troops at the beginning of the Second World War was extremely quick.

During late spring and early summer of 1940, the Germans pushed the French and British back to the North Sea.

The French and British made futile attempts to stop the advance but eventually found themselves at the French port of Dunkirk with nowhere left to retreat to except Britain.

What happened next was nothing short of a miracle.

The Germans stopped rather than force a final battle, and the British organized a fleet of ships to ferry the troops trapped on the beaches of Dunkirk over the sea to Britain.

This was the famous Dunkirk Evacuation plan.

British troops going home

Any ship that was seaworthy and many that were not, made their way across the short stretch of sea to Dunkirk. It was thought that about 40,000 men would be saved, but in fact, between May 26 and June 4, 1940, over 200,000 troops were transported back to Britain. More than 900 ships were used, and these included fishing boats, lifeboats, barges and pleasure crafts. Unfortunately, many were sunk.

Even though all of the heavy equipment was left behind, it was classed as a huge victory over the Germans and showed what could happen if everybody pulled together.

With France defeated by Germany, it was time for the Battle of Britain to begin.

The Battle of Britain

After the evacuation of troops off the beaches of Dunkirk, Britain stood alone in Europe. The Battle of Britain was one of the most significant of World War Two and was fought in the skies above Britain. Europe had been conquered, and Germany now wanted to take control of Britain. To do this, they knew that it was important to gain control of the air.

The Battle of Britain was the story of German aggression to destroy the Royal Air Force (RAF) and prepare for the invasion to take place. The first attack started on July 10, 1940.

German Heinkel bombers over Britain

Even though Germany had more planes, the RAF had Radar, so could mobilize their defenses according to where an attack took place.

The RAF continued to frustrate Hitler and forced him into making a fatal mistake. Even though it was taking a long time, the German tactic of bombing airfields was working. For no apparent reason, the Germans switched to attacking cities, like London, and this marked a turning point in the Battle of Britain.

An important date in the battle was September 15, 1940. The German Air Force launched a massive attack against London. The RAF was mobilized and shot down many German bombers. This made the German High Command realize that the British were still strong and far from being defeated.

The air raids continued, but it was slowly dawning on the Germans that they were fighting a losing battle.

Against the odds, the Battle of Britain was a decisive victory for Britain.

Trivia

The German air force was called the Luftwaffe.

The invasion of Britain was called Operation Sea Lion.

Over 1000 British planes were shot down during the battle, but almost 2000 German planes were destroyed.

The bombing of Britain lasted until May 1941 but gradually got less and less.

The Bombing ended because the bombers were needed for the Russian campaign

The War at Sea

Control of the sea was critical to the Allies and the Axis. Without the constant stream of supplies from America to Britain and Russia, the war would have been lost. The Allies were determined that supplies got through and the Axis forces were determined to stop them.

The conflict for control of the Atlantic Ocean is called the Battle of the Atlantic.

The battle was fought in the Northern Atlantic, though it spread rapidly as soon as America entered the war. The battle continued throughout the war and finally ended in 1945.

At the start of the war, the German U-Boats were very successful at sinking British ships. Because of the success of the submarines, the German government built many more. It was thought that they could force Britain to surrender by cutting off food and armaments.

The Allies countered the U-Boat attacks by traveling in heavily armed convoys. These were escorted by warships.

German U-Boat on patrol in the Atlantic

In 1943, there was a huge breakthrough by the Allies. They found-out the German attack codes so could listen in on messages. The allied ships also had radar to help find and destroy the U-Boats, and special underwater bombs.

Whoever gained control of the Atlantic would eventually win the war. In the end, the Allies gained control, but not without an enormous loss of life and ships. Both the Allies and the Axis had over 30,000 sailors killed. The Allies had 175 warships destroyed and 3,500 supply ships. The Germans had 783 U-Boats destroyed.

Trivia

Britain needed around 25 ships a day to get through the German blockade to continue fighting. It was a close thing, but they succeeded.

German submarines often traveled together in groups called 'Wolf Packs.'

Pearl Harbor

On December 7, 1941, the most infamous attack took place against the US Fleet stationed in Pearl Harbor. Planes from the Japanese Air Force attacked and destroyed a lot of American ships and killed many American sailors. Because of this event, America entered the war.

Pearl Harbor is situated in Hawaii on Oahu Island. At the time of the bombing, Hawaii was not a US State, but American territory.

Before the attack, the USA had remained neutral in the war in Europe and Asia.

Japan was continuing its policy of expansion and was worried that America would enter the war on the side of the Allies. They attacked to cause as much damage as possible in the hope that the American Navy would be so severely damaged that the US would not want war.

They could not have been more wrong. America declared war the next day.

USS Arizona on fire after the attack

This was a surprise attack involving hundreds of Japanese planes. The Japanese came to bomb the ships in two assault waves.

On December 8, 1941, America went to war against Japan.

Germany and Italy then declared war on the USA.

Even though the attack had caused a lot of damage, it was not as much as the Japanese had hoped for. A lot of facilities had been spared, which included depots for storing oil and repair yards.

There were no aircraft carriers in Pearl Harbour, which was important, as these ships would later become crucial in the war effort.

Trivia

It has been stated that the Japanese wanted to declare war before bombing Pearl Harbor, but the message didn't get through. This is, however, highly debatable.

The attack lasted 110 minutes.

The Battle of Stalingrad

The fight between the Germans and the Russians for control of Stalingrad marked the turning point in the war in Europe. The German defeat suffered here was devastating. So many German lives were lost in the freezing conditions that Germany never recovered.

The city is situated on the river Volga in Southwest Russia. At the time, Stalingrad was a major industrialized city and because of its railway connections, was highly strategic to whichever side controlled it.

German soldiers fighting in Stalingrad

The battle for the city commenced in the winter of 1942 and continued through January 1943. The Germans eventually surrendered in February 1943.

Like most German attack plans, the battle started with the Luftwaffe bombing the city. A large part of the city was destroyed and allowed the German troops to take control. However, the Russians didn't give up and continued to fight for every house and every street. Many German soldiers lost their lives in the ensuing struggle.

The Russian Army counter-attacked in November and trapped the German Army in the city. With food running out, and the bitterly cold conditions, most of the army surrendered.

Over 750,000 German troops died in Stalingrad and half a million Russians.

Trivia

Adolph Hitler was very angry that the German troops had surrendered. He wanted them to fight until death.

By reducing the city to rubble, the Germans made it much easier to defend. They could not use their tanks because of the destruction.

About 90,000 German troops were captured at Stalingrad.

D-Day

The Allies returned to Europe after the Dunkirk evacuation, on June 6, 1944. On this day a combined force of around 150,000 British, American and Canadian troops landed in Normandy, France. This was the famous D-Day landing that was the start of the push for victory against the Axis forces.

The preparation for the D-Day landings was extremely complicated to plan. It was to be a coordinated attack that used the Navy, Army, and Airforce. Before the landings, the German defenses were attacked by 1000 Allied bombers in an attempt to cause chaos.

The German command knew from intelligence information that an attack was coming, but they didn't know where. This meant that they could not concentrate their soldiers, and had to defend the whole coastline. The Allies tried to fool the Germans by sending out false information about where they would attack.

D-Day had taken many months of planning, but it was nearly called off because of adverse weather conditions. In fact, this worked in favor of the Allies. The German command thought that conditions were too dangerous for a sea landing and were not on full alert.

The attack began with paratroops landing behind enemy lines. The aim was to cause havoc and capture strategic targets such as bridges before the German troops could destroy them.

Bombers and warships, then attacked German soldiers, and French resistance agents cut telephone lines and sabotaged trains.

The arrival of 6,000 invasion ships marked the beginning of the assault and the beach landings. These ships carried soldiers, tanks, artillery, and equipment.

As D-Day drew to a close, the Allies had landed more than 150,000 troops on the beaches of Normandy. These soldiers began to battle their way inland, while more troops arrived. This was the beginning of the end, for the Axis Forces.

American Landing Barges off the coast of Normandy

Trivia

The attack was planned to take place during a full moon to allow troops to see mined obstacles in the surf.

D-Day was part of an overall operation that was called 'Operation Overlord.' The landing in Normandy was called 'Operation Neptune.'

The Battle of the Bulge

American Troops in the Ardennes

After the D-Day landings, the German troops were in continuous retreat. The Battle of the Bulge was an attempt to halt the advance. Most of the troops that engaged with the Germans were American.

The German counter attack started on December 16, 1944. The ensuing battle lasted for a month. German troops advanced through the Forest of the Ardennes in Belgium. The aim was to use 200,000 soldiers and 1000 tanks to break through the American front line.

Because it was winter and snowing, the Ardennes assault took the Americans completely by surprise.

German spies were parachuted behind American lines dressed like American soldiers. This was an attempt to cause confusion.

Due to the courageous fighting of small groups of American soldiers, they were able to hold the Germans up until reinforcements arrived. It was one of the biggest American victories of the Second World War and ultimately led to Germany's defeat.

Trivia

Winston Churchill said. "This is undoubtedly the greatest American battle of the war."

Another reason why the Germans lost this battle was because their tanks ran out of fuel.

More than 600,000 American soldiers fought in the Battle of the Bulge.

The Battle of Berlin

The last big battle of WW2 was the fight to take Berlin. This resulted in the German surrender and the death of Adolph Hitler, who committed suicide.

This battle commenced on April 16, 1945, and lasted until May 2, 1945.

A street in Berlin after the battle

The battle for Berlin was mainly between German forces and the Red Army (Soviet Union). The Germans were totally outnumbered by the Soviet army, which consisted of over two and a half million soldiers. The Soviets also had over 700 aircraft and 6,250 tanks.

Germany had a million troops, 2,200 aircraft, and 1,500 tanks. The German army consisted of not only regular soldiers but also young boys and old men. The Soviet troops quickly defeated the Germans defending Berlin, and they advanced into the city itself. Within days, the city was surrounded, and Hitler realized that it was only a matter of time. With the Soviet troops closing in on the city center, Hitler committed suicide.

On May 2, 1945, the German generals left in the city, surrendered to the Soviet commanders. WW2 ultimately ended May 8,1945.

The war was finally over in Europe.

The war had left Berlin in ruins and millions of Germans without homes.

The Battle of Midway

The war against the Japanese meant that America had to divide its troops between Europe and the Pacific. The Battle of Midway was a crucial victory and was a turning point. It started on June 4, 1942, and finished June 7, 1942. Midway is an island situated between America and Asia. It is about two and a half thousand miles from Japan. The island was considered strategically important to Japan and America.

After the USA attacked some of the Japanese 'home islands.' The Japanese decided to launch an attack on the US base on the island of Midway.

The USS Yorktown burning after Japanese Attack

The Japanese tried yet another surprise attack, but this time the Americans were ready. US code breakers had intercepted Japanese secret transmissions about the raid. This meant that before the attack, they already knew about it and could prepare.

On July 4, the Japanese began the attack with bombers, launched from aircraft carriers.

While the Japanese attacked Midway, American torpedo bombers attacked their ships. Four aircraft carriers were sunk.

The Yorktown (US aircraft carrier) attacked the last Japanese carrier, the Hiryu. In the fight that followed both were sunk.

Trivia

The loss of the aircraft carriers was a huge blow to the Japanese. They would never recover from it.

This was a major Allied Victory, and the beginning of the end for Japan.

Midway today is considered to be American territory.

The Battle of Guadalcanal

This campaign was one of the most important in the war between America and Japan. This was the first time that the Americans began the offensive and attacked Japanese positions. The attack on Guadalcanal started on August 7, 1942, and continued for six months.

The region where this battle took place is an island situated to the north of Australia. Guadalcanal is part of the Solomon Islands that are located in the South Pacific.

After the attack on Pearl Harbor, the Japanese had advanced through much of the South Pacific and were now threatening Australia. It had taken time for the Americans to build up enough forces to launch a counter attack. By August 1942, they decided to attack Guadalcanal.

The attack took the Japanese by surprise.

US Marines on patrol in Guadalcanal

The Japanese troops were naturally good at fighting in the jungle, and the battle for control of the island was not a foregone conclusion.

After an attack by the Japanese had been beaten back by Marines in November 1942, the battle began to turn in favor of America.

By February 1943, the US had complete control of the island.

Guadalcanal was significant because it marked the first time the Japanese Army had been stopped and made to retreat. This battle had the effect of demoralizing the Japanese and lifting the spirits of American troops.

The Japanese had 38 ships sunk and 31,000 soldiers killed. The Allies lost 29 ships and just over 7000 soldiers.

Trivia

The battle codename was Operation Watchtower

The Japanese reinforcement convoys that arrived during the night were nicknamed by American troops the Tokyo Express.

Many Japanese soldiers died from starvation and disease during the campaign.

The Battle of Iwo Jima

Americans raise the flag on Iwo Jima

The Battle of Iwo Jima was the first to take place on Japanese home soil. The island was important to the Americans because of its airfield. This would allow US airplanes to land and takeoff when attacking targets in Japan.

The island of Iwo Jima is not very big and is located just over 700 miles off the southern coast of Japan. Most of the island is completely flat.

US Marines landed on the island on February 19, 1945. The Japanese defended the island with a ferociousness that surprised US commanders. They thought that the battle would be over in a few days, but it took more than a month.

The Japanese used secret tunnels to harass American troops, which made advancing very dangerous. The island was finally made secure by the Americans and the flag raised above the only high ground, Mount Suribachi. The picture of the flag being raised is one of the most famous taken during the war.

Trivia

More Americans were wounded during the battle, but there were more Japanese killed. This was because the Japanese troops had been ordered to fight to the death. Because of this, only 216 were taken, prisoner.

Just over 6000 Americans died during the battle.

To defend the island, the Japanese had dug over eleven miles of secret tunnels.

The Atomic Bomb

Codenamed the Manhattan Project, the Americans developed the first atomic bomb as the ultimate weapon. Tests were carried out in the desert of New Mexico and showed how powerful the atomic bomb was. Germany surrendered before it could be used, but Japan would not surrender.

The decision to drop the bomb on Hiroshima and Nagasaki was taken to save the lives of American soldiers that would have died if mainland Japan was attacked.

Enola Gay was the B-29 plane that dropped the first atomic bomb

Six days after the terrifying explosion that destroyed Nagasaki, Emperor Hirohito went on Japanese radio to announce the surrender. Most Japanese had never heard his voice before.

Trivia

The principal scientist on Project Manhattan was JR Oppenheimer. He is often referred to as the 'Father of the atomic bomb.'

A bomb made from uranium was dropped on Hiroshima, and a plutonium bomb was dropped on Nagasaki.

The Aftermath of War

The war had the effect of changing a lot of Europe and Asia, especially the borders of countries that had been invaded

In Europe

Germany had controlled a lot of Europe during the war years. After the war, Germany was divided into East and West. The East came under Soviet control and the West under America, Britain, and France.

The Soviet Union also didn't want to give up the land taken in its advance on Germany. For many years Czechoslovakia, Hungary, Albania, Bulgaria, Romania and Poland became 'buffer' states between the USSR and the West.

Aid was given to Europe by America and outlined in the Marshall Plan to help it rebuild.

In Asia

After the war, Allied forces occupied Japan. The country did not get its independence back until 1952.

Korea was divided into North and South.

A civil war raged in China between the communists and the nationalists, which the communists won. Most of the nationalists left China for Taiwan.

War Crimes

Many leaders in Japan and Germany stood trial after the war for war crimes that had been committed. These were acts that were deemed illegal under the Geneva Convention. Crimes included the holocaust, torture and slave labor. Many of the prominent leaders of the Axis were executed for crimes against humanity.

The United Nations

After the problems caused by the Treaty of Versailles, the Allies were well aware that there was a possibility of World War Three unless they did something to stop it. Formed in October 1945, the United Nations had 51 members. These included five nations that made up the Security Council. The five nations were America, Britain, The Soviet Union, France, and China.

The start of the Cold War

Post-1945, Europe was split into East and West. The East was controlled by Russia, and the West had at its head, the USA.

The West formed an alliance to fight the advance of communism. The Cold War never escalated into a real war, but it was to last for the next 45 years, with some moments of great tension between the 'Super Powers.'

Weird Facts about WW2

More than 100,000 bomber crewmen from the Allies were killed in operations over Europe.

More Americans died in the Air Corps than the Marines.

Every British soldier was issued with three sheets of toilet paper a day. Every American got 22!

Four out of every five of the Axis forces were killed on the Eastern Front in Russia.

Americans didn't want to eat hamburgers during the war because they sounded too German. Hamburgers were renamed Liberty Stakes.

The nephew of Adolph Hitler served in the American Navy during the war.

The first bomb dropped on Berlin killed an elephant in the zoo

The Americans had targeted Tokyo to drop the third atom bomb if necessary.

More people were killed in Russia than any other country. Over 21 million.

How much did you learn about WW2?

1 What date did Britain declare war on Germany?

2 What was the name of the British 'War' Prime Minister?

3 When did the Japanese Attack Pearl Harbor?

4 Which Allied troops fought in the Battle of the Bulge?

5 What was a Liberty Steak?

6 Which two countries fought in the Battle of Iwo Jima?

7 What was Enola Gay?

8 What is significant about May 2, 1945?

Thank You for Reading this Book

You can visit the English Reading Tree Page by clicking:

Visit Amazon's Keith Goodman Page

Books in the English Reading Tree Series by Keith Goodman include:

1 The Titanic for Kids

2 Shark Facts for Kids

3 Solar System Facts for Kids

4 Dinosaur Facts for Kids

5 American Facts and Trivia for Kids

6 Christmas Facts and Trivia for Kids

7 Space Race Facts for Kids

8 My Titanic Adventure for Kids

9 Save the Titanic for Kids

10 Halloween Facts and Trivia for Kids

11 Discovering Ancient Egypt for Kids

12 Native American Culture for Kids

Made in the USA
Las Vegas, NV
16 May 2022